Saints of Christmas
Activity Book

- For ages 4-9
- Reproducible pages
- Saddle-stitched for easy copying

Katherine A. Borgatti

SAINTS • OF • CHRISTMAS

Saints AND me!

Liguori

ONE LIGUORI DRIVE
LIGUORI MO 63057-9999

Imprimi Potest:
Harry Grile, CSsR, Provincial
Denver Province, The Redemptorists

Published by Liguori Publications
Liguori, Missouri 63057

To order, call 800-325-9521
www.liguori.org

p ISBN 978-0-7648-2365-7
e ISBN 978-0-7648-6851-1

Liguori Publications, a nonprofit corporation, is an apostolate of The Redemptorists. To learn more about The Redemptorists, visit Redemptorists.com.

Printed in the United States of America
17 16 15 14 13 / 5 4 3 2 1
First Edition

How to Use This Book

This book contains reproducible coloring and activity pages to reinforce the six stories of the seven saints in the *Saints and Me!* series, *Saints of Christmas*: Martin de Porres, Nicholas of Myra, Lucy, Francis of Assisi, Mary and Joseph, and Gianna Beretta Molla. Use each page about these saints as a single lesson or all together to create hours of entertainment for children. Photocopy pages for use at home or in the classroom. Answer keys are provided in the back. After an activity is done, ask the kids to color them in!

spot the Difference

Spot 6 things that are different.

St. Martin could use your help finding his way to the end of this maze.

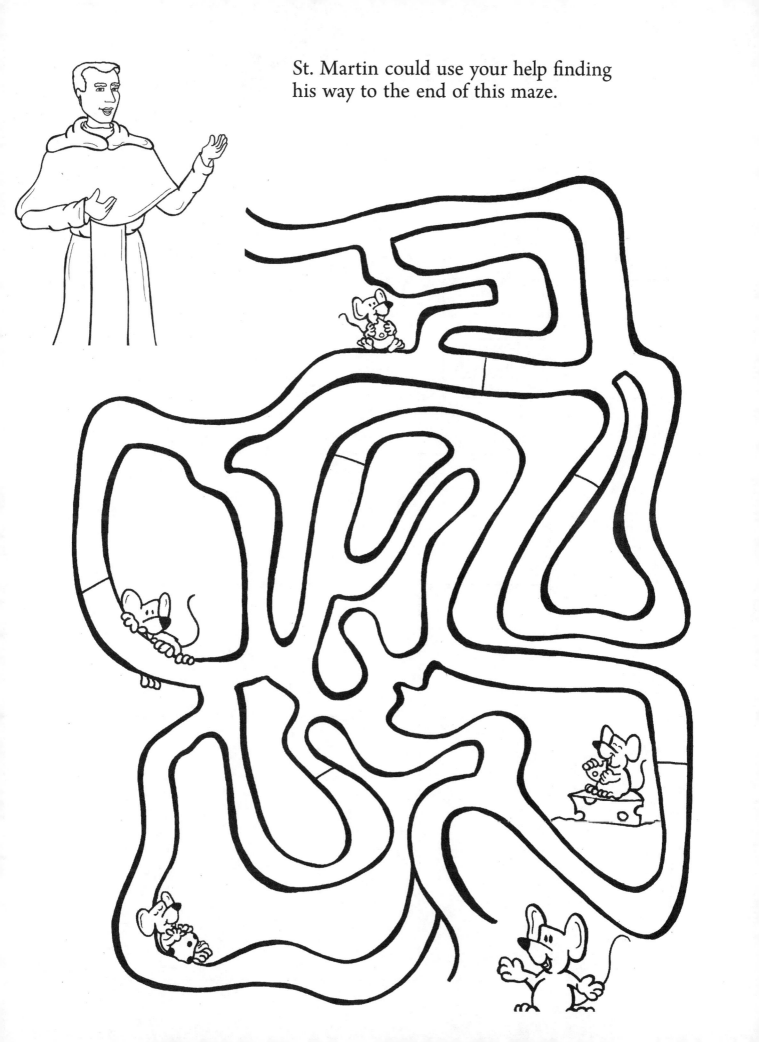

DRAW the saint

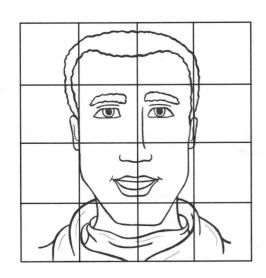

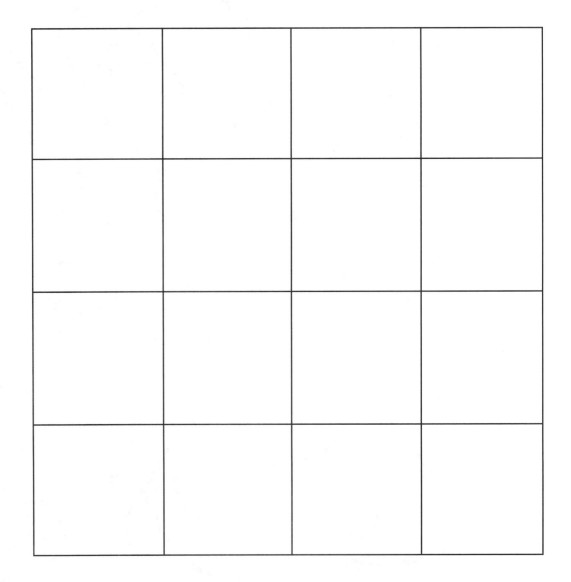

MOUSE·TAC·TOE

Have a little mousy fun and play some tic-tac-toe.

word search

Circle these 8 words. Remember, the words can be upside down or backward, as well as straight across.

Martin	Monastery	Helper	Blanket
Mouse	Peru	Brother	Orphanage

```
M  A  R  T  I  N  K  O
O  M  O  U  S  E  F  R
N  B  M  K  I  T  D  P
A  R  E  P  L  E  H  H
S  E  F  E  H  K  R  A
T  H  N  R  X  N  I  N
E  T  C  U  I  A  R  A
R  O  F  S  C  L  A  G
Y  R  J  D  X  B  C  E
A  B  J  L  P  U  R  W
```

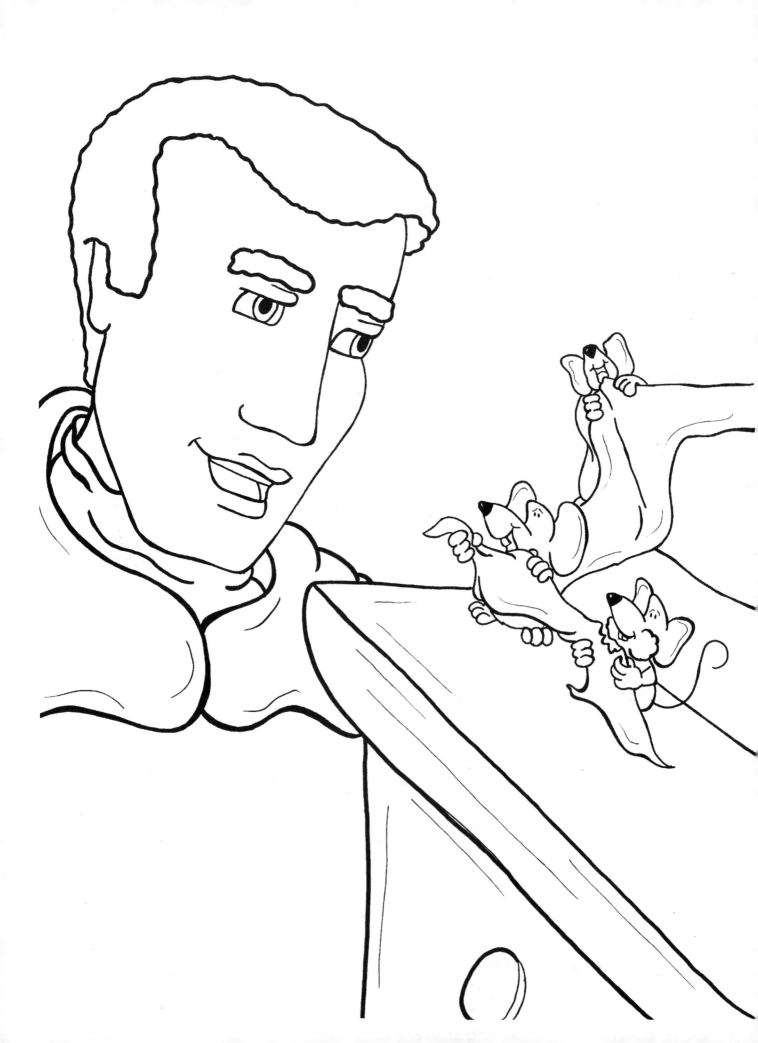

snow Day

Can you help this little mouse get ready to play in the snow?
Color and cut out the things he will need, like a hat, a scarf,
and a couple of snacks. Glue them on, and he's ready to go
have fun in the snow.

Tiny stars are sprinkled around,
circle each one until 12 are found.

Draw the saint

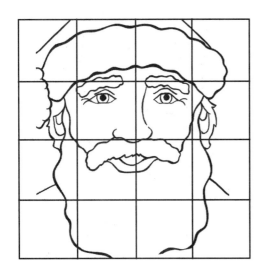

Draw what you see in each square to make a picture of St. Nicholas.

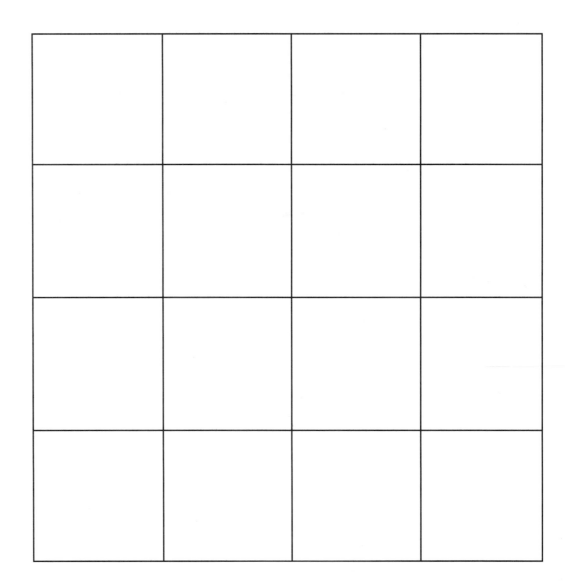

Help St. Nicholas find his way to the pile of coins.

CUT OUT

St. Nicholas has an empty bag, but
you can fill it right up.
Color these items and cut them out
to paste into St. Nicholas' bag.

Tic·Tac·gingerbread

Spice up these gingerbread people with X's and O's in a friendly game of tic-tac-toe.

Advent wreath

Make a beautiful Advent wreath. Color three candles purple, one candle pink, the leaves a pretty shade of green, and the bow a bright red to complete this scene. Hint: Add a little yellow glitter to the flames to make your candles shine.

DRAW the saint

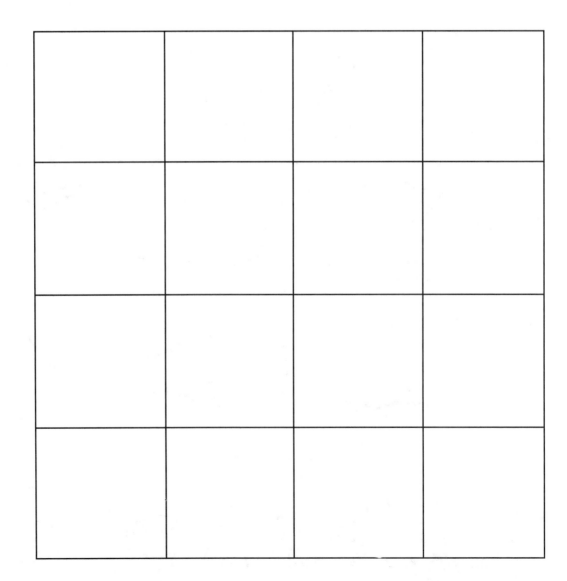

make a christmas snow globe

Draw your favorite things about Christmas
inside the circle of the snow globe.
Color it in, and then add your own snow
on top. Glitter makes pretty snow. So do
little pieces of cotton balls rolled into tiny
snowballs. Be creative!

connect the Dots

unscramble the words

These words are all mixed up.
Can you help me unscramble them?
If you need help, remember you can use
the word bank.

CLUY _____

ILIYSC _____

GTLIH _____

YESE _____

LENDAC _____

LHYO _____

WORD BANK:

EYES   HOLY   CANDLE
SICILY   LUCY   LIGHT

DRAW THE SAINT

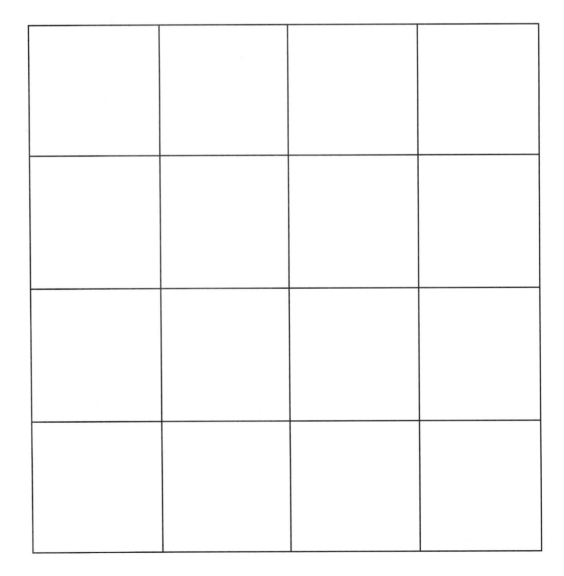

word search

Hoot hoot…Can you help me find these words?
Circle them as you find them.

WORD BANK:

FRANCIS
NATIVITY
CHRISTMAS
ANIMALS
SAINT
KNIGHT

H K O S T L P N Q
C A N I M A L S R
T V O T S Y X L S
D A S Y R L T A M
S O I T V K M N S
B K C I F T P C V
T B N V S A I N T
K P A I O V Z D G
L R R T G F S E H
A H F A T H M J K
C F X N S L T I L

finish the Drawing

These little snails need your help to finish this drawing. The tree stump, the grass, a flower, and the little snail's shell all need to be filled in.

unscramble the words

These words are all mixed up.
Can you help me unscramble them?

NCRAIG _____

KONM _____

SIASIS _____

YALTI _____

IRFAR _____

VADTNE _____

WORD BANK:

MONK
ITALY
ADVENT
FRIAR
CARING
ASSISI

Fill in the Facts

Help me fill out my story by writing the answers in the blanks.

My name is _____.

I was born in _____,_____.

_____ is my feast day.

I am the patron saint of

_____,_____, and

_____.

WORD BANK:

ASSISI
ST. FRANCIS
ITALY
ANIMALS
NATURE
OCTOBER 4
ITALY

DRAW the saint

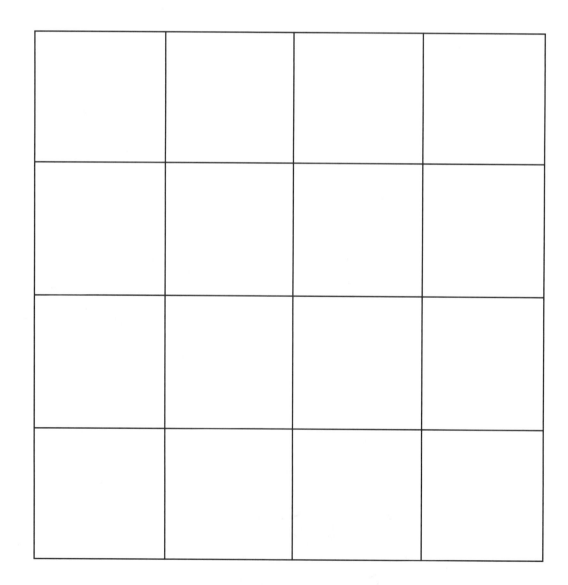

connect the DOts

Connect the dots to make a pretty Christmas candle.
Remember to color your beautiful picture.

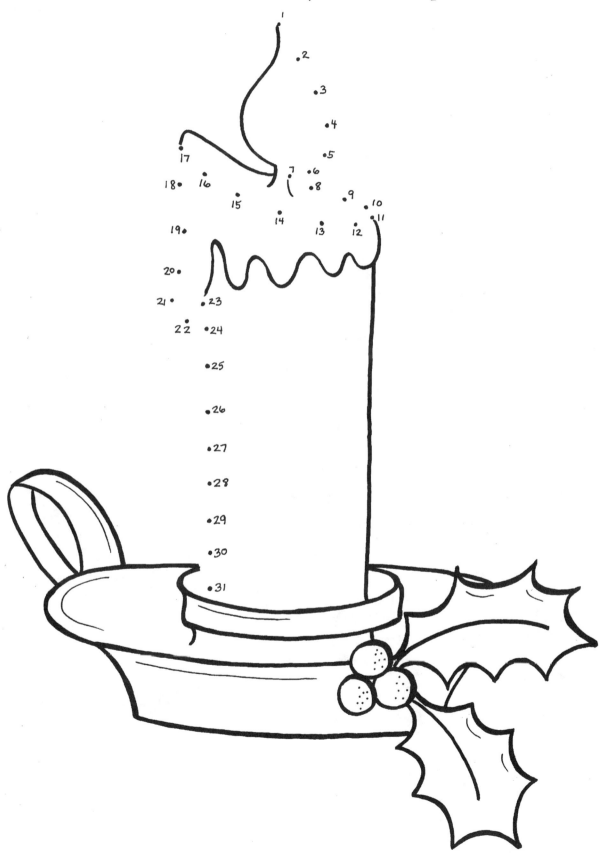

Which way should the wise men go?
Help them find their way to the shining star.

This little snowman is missing a few things.
He needs two eyes, a carrot nose, a happy smile,
some arms, and a little decoration on his scarf.

scavenger hunt

Have fun finding these items:
1 ruler   4 tacks
2 hammers   5 silly birds
3 saws

DRAW the saint

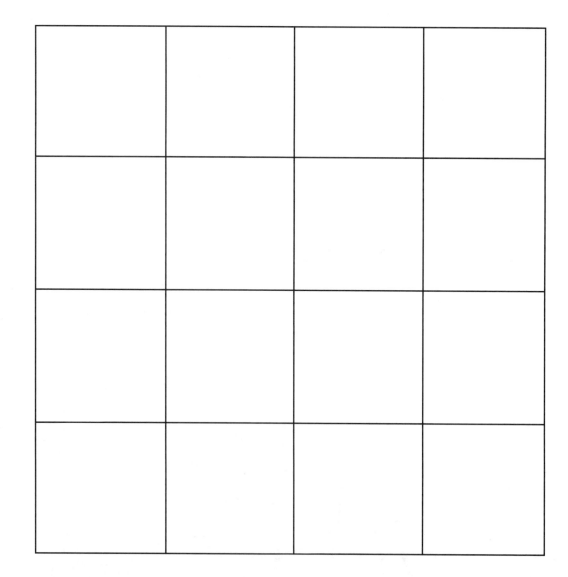

DRAW the saint

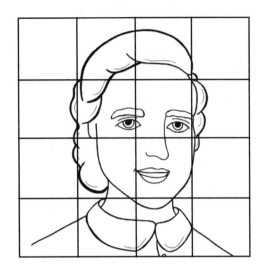

connect the Dots

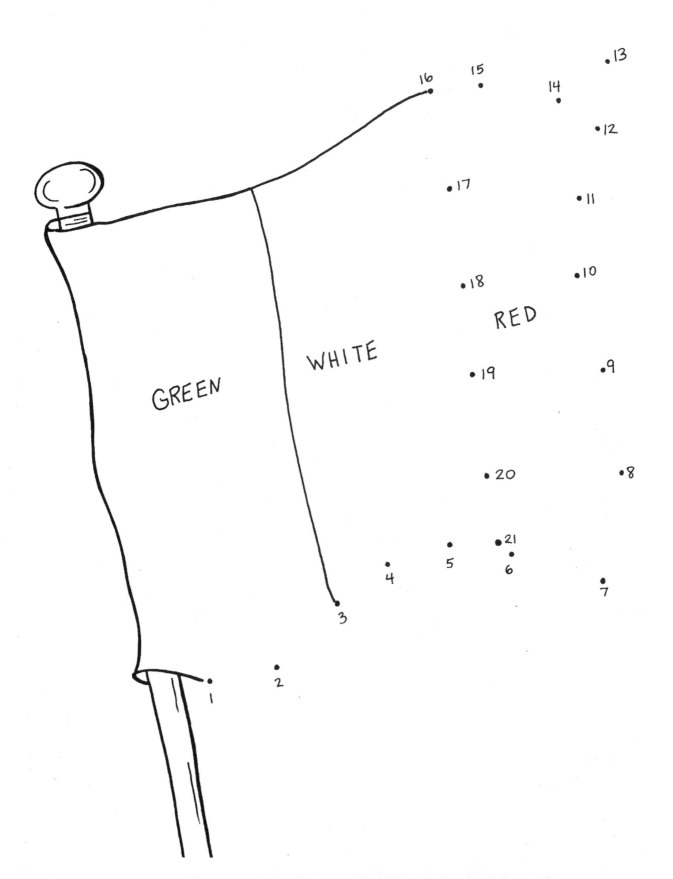

Picnic Pursuit

Hmmm....
I'm going on a picnic, and I'm not sure what to bring. Circle the things that I should pack in my picnic basket.

SANDWICH

PAINT BRUSH

HUNGRY ANT

ORANGE JUICE

CRAB WITH A CHEF HAT

WATERMELON

FORK AND SPOON

SPOOL OF THREAD

BLANKET

INCH WORM

COOKIES

COFFEE CUP

SPOT the DIFFERENCE

Can you spot and circle 8 things that make
these pictures different from one another?

unscramble the words

These words are all mixed up.
Can you help me unscramble them?

RODOTC _____

NAINGA _____

YLTIA _____

EHOMRT _____

RYPAER _____

IMLYFA _____

WORD BANK:

MOTHER   DOCTOR
FAMILY   GIANNA
ITALY   PRAYER

Spot the Difference

Spot 6 things that are different.

St. Martin could use your help finding his way to the end of this maze.

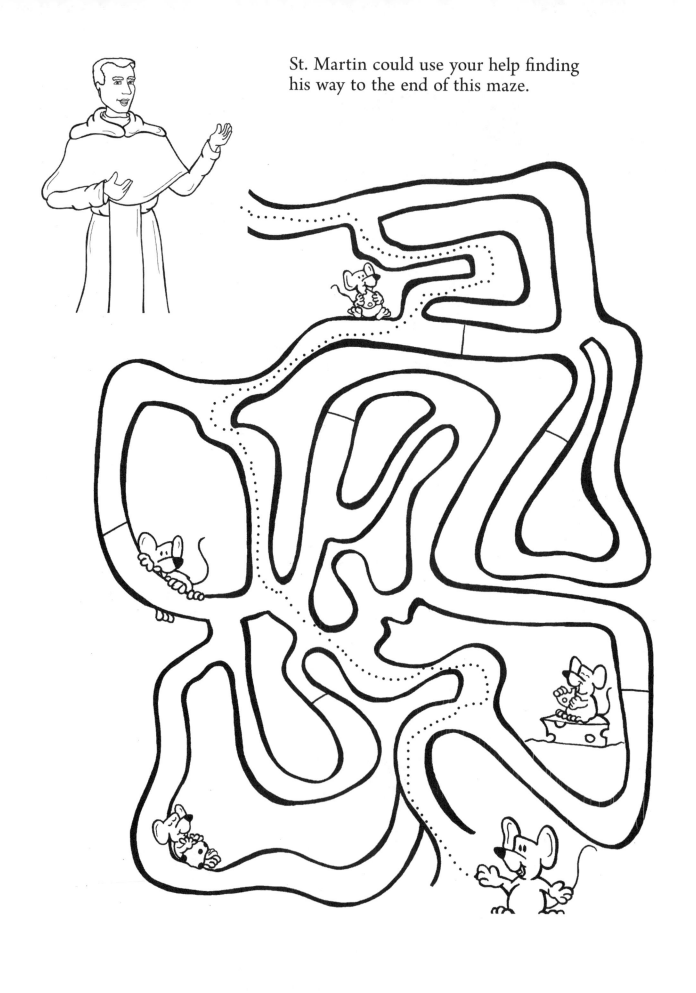

word search

Circle these 8 words. Remember, the words can be upside down or backward, as well as straight across.

| Martin | Monastery | Helper | Blanket |
| Mouse | Peru | Brother | Orphanage |

```
M  A  R  T  I  N  K     O
O  M  O  U  S  E  F     R
N  B  M  K  I  T  D     P
A  R  E  P  L  E  H     H
S  E  F  E  H  K  R     A
T  H  N  R  X  N  I     N
E  T  C  U  I  A  R     A
R  O  F  S  C  L  A     G
Y  R  J  D  X  B  C     E
A  B  J  L  P  U  R     W
```

Tiny stars are sprinkled around,
circle each one until 12 are found.

Help St. Nicholas find his way
to the pile of coins

connect the Dots

unscramble the words

These words are all mixed up. Can you help me unscramble them? If you need help, remember you can use the word bank.

CLUY	LUCY
ILIYSC	SICILY
GTLIH	LIGHT
YESE	EYES
LENDAC	CANDLE
LHYO	HOLY

WORD BANK:

EYES	HOLY	CANDLE
SICILY	LUCY	LIGHT

word search

Hoot hoot...Can you help me find these words?
Circle them as you find them.

WORD BANK:

FRANCIS
NATIVITY
CHRISTMAS
ANIMALS
SAINT
KNIGHT

H K O S T L P N Q
C A N I M A L S R
T V O T S Y X L S
D A S Y R L T A M
S O I T V K M N S
B K C I F T P C V
T B N V S A I N T
K P A I O V Z D G
L R R T G F S E H
A H F A T H M J K
C F X N S L T I L

unscramble the words

These words are all mixed up.
Can you help me unscramble them?

NCRAIG	CARING
KONM	MONK
SIASIS	ASSISI
YALTI	ITALY
IRFAR	FRIAR
VADTNE	ADVENT

WORD BANK:

MONK
ITALY
ADVENT
FRIAR
CARING
ASSISI

Fill in the Facts

Help me fill out my story by writing the answers in the blanks.

My name is <u>ST. FRANCIS</u>.

I was born in <u>ASSISI, ITALY</u>.

<u>OCTOBER 4</u> is my feast day.

I am the patron saint of

<u>ANIMALS</u>, <u>NATURE</u>, and

<u>ITALY</u>.

WORD BANK:

ASSISI
ST. FRANCIS
ITALY
ANIMALS
NATURE
OCTOBER 4
ITALY

connect the Dots

Connect the dots to make a pretty Christmas candle.
Remember to color your beautiful picture.

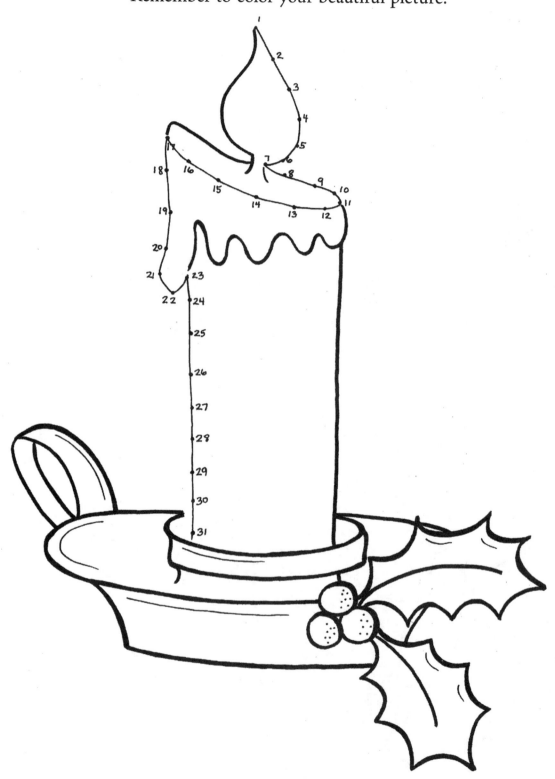

Which way should the wise men go?
Help them find their way to the shining star.

scavenger hunt

Have fun finding these items:

1 ruler   4 tacks
2 hammers   5 silly birds
3 saws

connect the dots

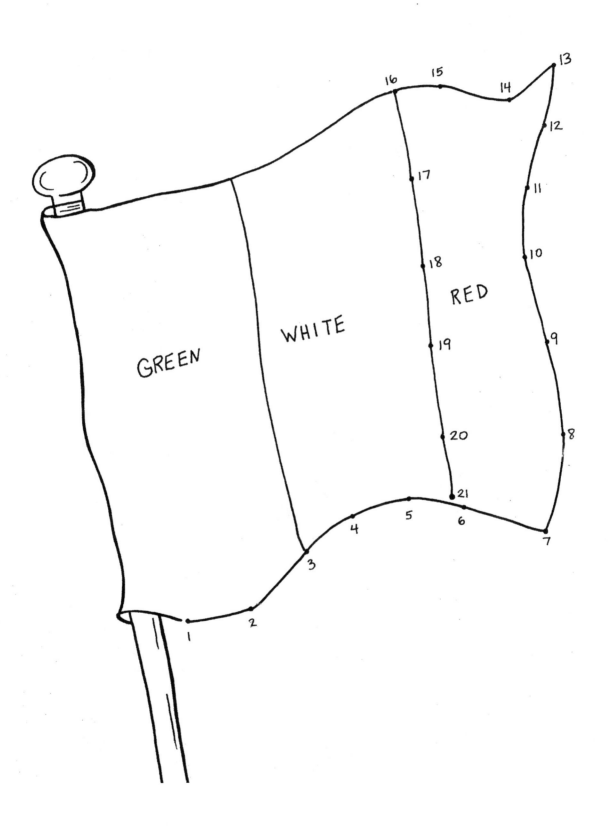

picnic pursuit

Hmmm....
I'm going on a picnic, and I'm not sure what to bring. Circle the things that I should pack in my picnic basket.

SANDWICH

PAINT BRUSH

HUNGRY ANT

ORANGE JUICE

CRAB WITH A CHEF HAT

WATERMELON

FORK AND SPOON

SPOOL OF THREAD

BLANKET

INCH WORM

COOKIES

COFFEE CUP

SPOT the DiFFERENCE

Can you spot and circle 8 things that make these pictures different from one another?

unscramble the words

These words are all mixed up.
Can you help me unscramble them?

RODOTC   DOCTOR

NAINGA   GIANNA

YLTIA   ITALY

EHOMRT   MOTHER

RYPAER   PRAYER

IMLYFA   FAMILY

WORD BANK:

MOTHER   DOCTOR
FAMILY   GIANNA
ITALY   PRAYER

About the Author

Katherine Alpha Borgatti is an artist and illustrator native to Louisiana. She is a convert to the Catholic faith and has a passion for Catholic art. Her works include portraits of Jesus, the Blessed Virgin Mary, and various saints. Katherine has painted a variety of murals, including one for the Louisiana Children's Discovery Center in Hammond, Louisiana. In May of 2010 she completed a children's book that she wrote, illustrated, and published through her company, Painted Daisies Inc.: *Imagination Created*. The slogan "Imagination Created" is designed to encompass the idea that if you can imagine it, we can create it, she says. She also donates her talent to the Catholic church and school that her children attend and visits local schools to do book readings and signings. Katherine lives in Mandeville, Louisiana, with her husband, Mike, and their three children, Matthew, Annamarie, and John.

Brother Francis • Faith-Building DVDs, Books, and More!

Enjoy the sound teaching and great quality entertainment this series offers.

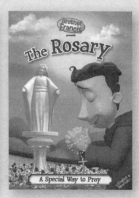

Let's Pray!
A Lesson on Prayer

This wonderfully fun episode will encourage children to pray and establish a personal relationship with God. Includes:

- "The Sign of the Cross" and "The Our Father"
- *Two visualized songs*
  "Let's Pray" and "With God's Love"
- *Featured story*
  The Little Way of Saint Therese

Bilingual DVD
501360 • **$12.99**

The Bread of Life
Celebrating the Eucharist

An inspirational and instructive presentation that teaches children all about the Sacrament of the Eucharist and prepares them for their first Holy Communion. Includes:

- "The Last Supper"
- *Two visualized songs*
  "I am the Bread of Life" and "What More Could He Give?"
- *Featured story*
  The Story of Blessed Imelda Lambertini

Bilingual DVD
501391 • **$12.99**

The Rosary
A Special Way to Pray

Join Brother Francis in this entertaining and guidance-filled presentation that will inspire children to deepen their faith by praying the Rosary. Includes

- The Prayers of the Rosary
- The Apostles' Creed
- *Two visualized songs*
  "I Love to Pray" and "The Our Father"
- *Featured story*
  The Annunciation

Bilingual DVD
501432 • **$12.99**

Forgiven
The Blessings of Confession

This joyful presentation reminds old and young alike about the great gift of God's forgiveness through the Sacrament of Reconciliation. Includes

- How to make a good confession
- *Two visualized songs*
  "God is a Loving Father" and "Praise God, I'm Forgiven."
- *Featured story*
  The Parable of the Tax Collector

Bilingual DVD
501460 • **$12.99**

Born into the Kingdom
The Miracle of Baptism

In this happy presentation, Brother Francis invites us to share in the realities of the Sacrament of Baptism and the union it provides us with God's big family! Includes:

- How We Celebrate the Sacrament of Baptism
- *Two visualized songs*
  "I've Got a Family" and "Jesus is the Light of the World"
- *Featured story*
  The story of Adam and Eve

Bilingual DVD
015064 • **$12.99**

Coloring and Activity Books

A great way to help children review the many lessons found in each "Brother Francis" episode. They'll love the coloring pages, dot-to-dots, mazes, hidden-picture games, and activities in each book!

Let's Pray!
16 pages; 8.5 x 11
809630 • **$1.99**

The Bread of Life
16 pages; 8.5 x 11
809609 • **$1.99**

The Rosary
16 pages; 8.5 x 11
809616 • **$1.99**

Forgiven!
16 pages; 8.5 x 11
809647 • **$1.99**

The Miracle of Baptism
16 pages; 8.5 x 11
809692 • **$1.99**